WILDLIFE VIEWING AREAS

Nebraska Ecoregions

- High Plains
- Northwestern Glaciated Plains
- Nebraska Sand Hills
- Central Great Plains
- Northwestern Great Plains
- Western Corn Belt Plains

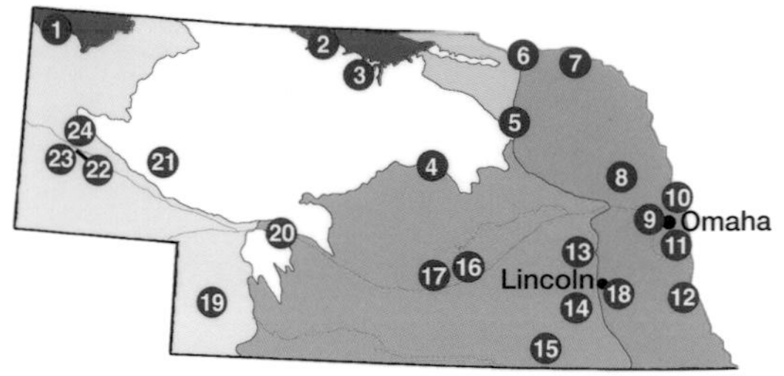

1. Oglala National Grassland
2. Fort Niobrara National Wildlife Refuge
3. Long Lake State Recreation Area
4. Pibel Lake State Recreation Area
5. Pierson Wildlife Museum Learning Center
6. Bazile Creek Wildlife Management Area
7. Wiseman State Wildlife Management Area
8. Powderhorn State Wildlife Management Area
9. Neale Woods Nature Center
10. DeSoto National Wildlife Refuge
11. Fontenelle Forest Nature Center
12. River Country Nature Center
13. Pioneer Park Nature Center
14. Spring Creek Prairie Audubon Center
15. Rock Creek Station State Historical Park
16. Nebraska Nature & Visitor Center
17. Iain Nicolson Audubon Center at Rowe Sanctuary
18. University of Nebraska State Museum
19. Enders Reservoir State Recreation Area
20. Buffalo Bill Ranch State Recreation Area
21. Crescent Lake National Wildlife Refuge
22. Wildcat Hills Nature Center
23. Wyobraska Wildlife Museum
24. Stateline Islands Waterfowl Management Area

Most illustrations show the adult male in breeding coloration. Colors and markings may be duller or absent during different seasons. The measurements denote the length of species from nose/bill to tail tip. Butterfly measurements denote wingspan. Illustrations are not to scale.

Waterford Press produces reference guides that introduce novices to nature, science, travel and languages. Product information and hundreds of educational games are featured on the website: **www.waterfordpress.com**

To order, call 800-434-2555.
For permissions, or to share comments, e-ma
editor@waterfordpress.com. For information o
custom-published products, call 800-434-255
or e-mail info@waterfordpress.com.

140711

Scan for more info

ISBN 978-1-58355-694-8 $7.95 U.S 50795
9 781583 556948
UPC 8 84682 01049 2

NEBRASKA WILDLIFE – A Folding Pocket Guide to Familiar Animals

Kavanagh/Leung

A POCKET NATURALIST® GUIDE

NEBRASKA WILDLIFE

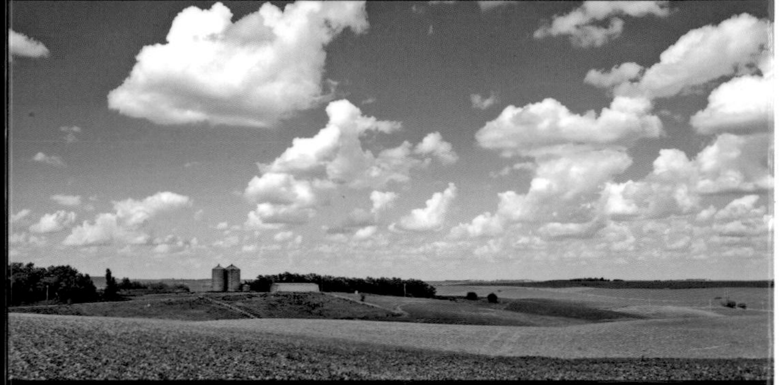

A Folding Pocket Guide to Familiar Animals

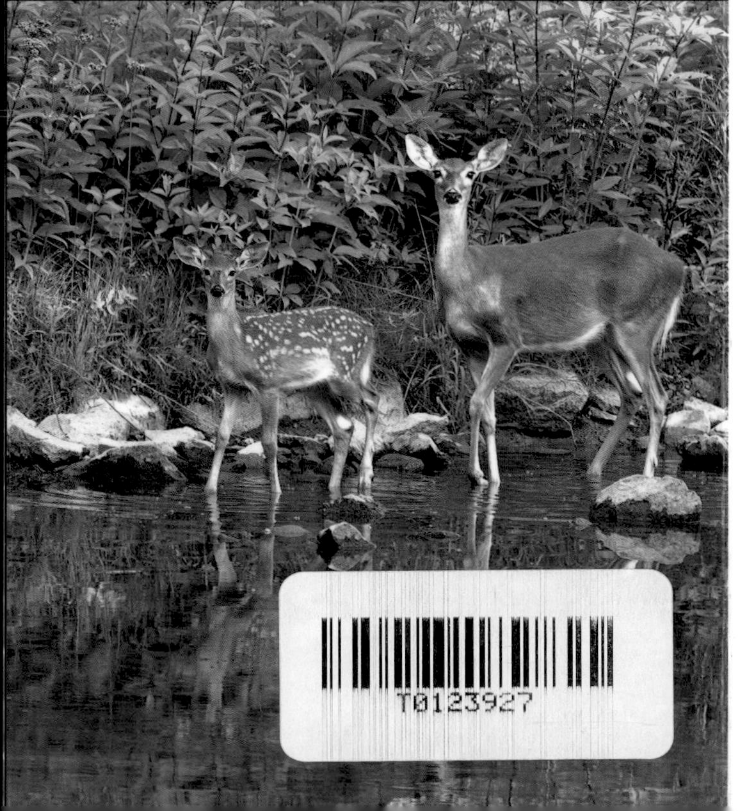

T0123927

INSECTS & INVERTEBRATES

Honey Bee
Apis mellifera
To .75 in. (2 cm)
Slender bee has pollen baskets on its rear legs. Can only sting once. **Nebraska's state insect.**

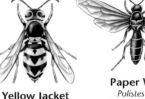

Yellow Jacket
Vespula pensylvanica
To .63 in. (1.6 cm)
Aggressive picnic pest can sting repeatedly.

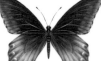

Paper Wasp
Polistes spp.
To 1 in. (3 cm)
Told by slender profile and dark, pale-banded abdomen. Builds papery hanging nests. Can sting repeatedly.

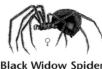

Bumble Bee
Bombus spp.
To 1 in. (3 cm)
Stout, furry bee is large and noisy. Can sting repeatedly.

Black Widow Spider
Latrodectus mactans
To .5 in. (1.3 cm)
Venomous spider has a red hourglass marking on its abdomen.

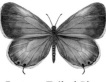

Ladybug
Adalia spp.
To .25 in. (.6 cm)

Black-and-yellow Garden Spider
Argiope aurantia
To 1.25 in. (3.2 cm)

Pond Crayfish
Procambarus spp.
To 5 in. (13 cm)

Water Strider
Gerris remigis
To .5 in. (1.3 cm)

Tiger Beetle
Cicindela spp.
To 1 in. (3 cm)

Whirligig Beetle
Family Gyrinidae
To .5 in. (1.3 cm)
Large swarms swirl around together on the water's surface.

Dragonfly
Suborder Epiprocta
To 3 in. (8 cm)
Most dragonflies rest with their wings held open.

Field Cricket
Gryllus pennsylvanicus
To 1 in. (3 cm)
Song is a series of three chirps.

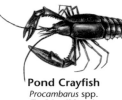

Cicada
Tibicen spp.
To 1.5 in. (4 cm)
Song is a sudden loud whine or buzz, maintained steadily before dying away.

Damselfly
Suborder Zygoptera
To 2 in. (5 cm)
Most damselflies rest with their wings held together over their back.

BUTTERFLIES & MOTHS

Pipevine Swallowtail
Battus philenor
To 3.5 in. (9 cm)

Common Sulphur
Colias philodice
To 2 in. (5 cm)
Common in open areas and along roadsides.

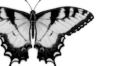

Eastern Tiger Swallowtail
Pterourus glaucus
To 6 in. (15 cm)

Eastern Tailed Blue
Everes comyntas
To 1 in. (3 cm)
Note orange spots above thread-like hindwing tails.

Cabbage White
Artogeia rapae
To 2 in. (5 cm)
One of the most common butterflies.

Monarch
Danaus plexippus
To 4 in. (10 cm)

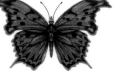

Viceroy
Basilarchia archippus
To 3 in. (8 cm)
Told from similar monarch by its smaller size and the thin, black band on its hindwings.

Red-spotted Purple
Basilarchia astyanax
To 3 in. (8 cm)

Great Spangled Fritillary
Speyeria cybele
To 3 in. (8 cm)
Common in marshes and wet meadows.

Buckeye
Junonia coenia
To 2.5 in. (6 cm)

Question Mark
Polygonia interrogationis
To 2.5 in. (6 cm)
Note lilac margin on wings. Silvery mark on underwings resembles a question mark or semi-colon.

American Snout
Libytheana carinenta
To 2 in. (5 cm)
'Snout' is formed from projecting mouth parts that enclose its coiled 'nose'.

Luna Moth
Actias luna
To 4.5 in. (11 cm)

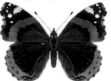

Red Admiral
Vanessa atalanta
To 2.5 in. (6 cm)

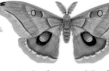

Polyphemus Moth
Antheraea polyphemus
To 6 in. (15 cm)

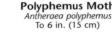

FISHES

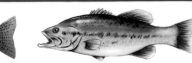

Rainbow Trout
Oncorhynchus mykiss To 44 in. (1.1 m)
Note reddish side stripe.

Largemouth Bass
Micropterus salmoides To 40 in. (1 m)
Note prominent side spots. Jaw joint extends past eye.

White Bass
Morone chrysops To 18 in. (45 cm)
Silvery fish has 4-7 dark side stripes.

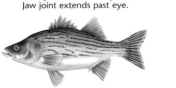

Hybrid Bass (Wiper)
Morone hybrid To 20 in. (50 cm)
Note broken side stripes. Striped and white bass hybrid is an aggressive sport fish.

Striped Bass
Morone saxatilis To 6 ft. (1.8 m)
Has 6-9 dark side stripes.

Black Crappie
Pomoxis nigromaculatus
To 16 in. (40 cm)

Paddlefish
Polyodon spathula To 7 ft. (2.1 m)
Has a long, paddle-shaped snout.

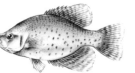

Bluegill
Lepomis macrochirus
To 16 in. (40 cm)

Northern Pike
Esox lucius To 53 in. (1.4 m)
Note large head and posterior dorsal fin. Has horizontal body spots.

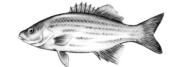

Pumpkinseed
Lepomis gibbosus
To 16 in. (40 cm)

Channel Catfish
Ictalurus punctatus To 4 ft. (1.2 m)
Note prominent 'whiskers'.
Nebraska's state fish.

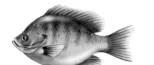

Walleye
Sander vitreus To 40 in. (1 m)
Note white spot on lower lobe of tail.

Shovelnose Sturgeon
Scaphirhynchus platorynchus
To 3 ft. (90 cm)
Note upturned snout.

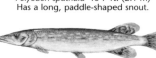

Yellow Perch
Perca flavescens
To 16 in. (40 cm)

REPTILES & AMPHIBIANS

Great Plains Toad
Bufo cognatus
To 4 in. (10 cm)
Call is a metallic trill.

Bullfrog
Lithobates catesbeiana
To 8 in. (20 cm)
Call is a deep-pitched – *jug-o-rum*.

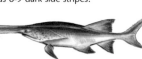

Western Chorus Frog
Pseudacris triseriata
To 1.5 in. (4 cm)
Note dark stripes on back. Call sounds like a thumbnail running over the teeth of a comb.

Northern Leopard Frog
Rana pipiens
To 4 in. (10 cm)
Brown to green frog has dark spots on its back. Call is a rattling snore with grunts and moans.

Tiger Salamander
Ambystoma tigrinum
To 13 in. (33 cm)

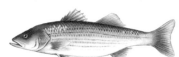

Eastern Fence Lizard
Sceloporus undulatus To 8 in. (20 cm)
Rough scaled. Has dark, zigzag bars down its back.

Snapping Turtle
Chelydra serpentina To 18 in. (45 cm)
Note knobby shell and long tail.

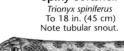

Eastern Painted Turtle
Trachemys picta picta
To 10 in. (25 cm)

Spiny Softshell
Trionyx spiniferus
To 18 in. (45 cm)
Note tubular snout.

Common Garter Snake
Thamnophis sirtalis sirtalis
To 4 ft. (1.2 m)
Note yellowish back stripe.

Gopher Snake
Pituophis catenifer To 8 ft. (2.4 m)
Note pointed snout.

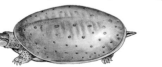

Northern Water Snake
Nerodia sipedon To 4.5 ft. (1.4 m)
Note dark blotches on back.

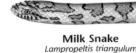

Milk Snake
Lampropeltis triangulum
To 7 ft. (2.1 m)

Prairie Rattlesnake
Crotalus viridis
To 5 ft. (1.5 m)
Venomous snake has a spade-shaped head.

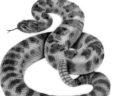

Canada Goose
Branta canadensis
To 45 in. (1.14 m)

Wood Duck
Aix sponsa
To 20 in. (50 cm)

Snow Goose
Chen caerulescens
To 31 in. (78 cm)

Mallard
Anas platyrhynchos
To 28 in. (70 cm)

Northern Shoveler
Anas clypeata To 20 in. (50 cm)
Named for its large spatulate bill.

Canvasback
Aythya valisineria To 2 ft. (60 cm)
Note sloping forehead and black bill.

Redhead
Aythya americana
To 22 in. (55 cm)

Common Merganser
Mergus merganser To 27 in. (68 cm)
Note slender profile and thin red bill.

Blue-winged Teal
Anas discors To 16 in. (40 cm)

Common Goldeneye
Bucephala clangula
To 20 in. (50 cm)

Northern Pintail
Anas acuta To 29 in. (73 cm)

Sandhill Crane
Grus canadensis
To 4 ft. (1.2 m)
Up to half a million cranes stage along the Platte River in spring.

Great Blue Heron
Ardea herodias
To 4.5 ft. (1.4 m)

American White Pelican
Pelecanus erythrorhynchos
To 5 ft. (1.5 m)

Ring-billed Gull
Larus delawarensis
To 20 in. (50 cm)
Bill has dark ring.

Double-crested Cormorant
Phalacrocorax auritus
To 3 ft. (90 cm)

Upland Sandpiper
Bartramia longicauda
To 12 in. (30 cm)
Note small head and long tail.

Mourning Dove
Zenaida macroura
To 13 in. (33 cm)
Call is a mournful –
ooah-woo-woo-woo.

Ruby-throated Hummingbird
Archilochus colubris
To 3.5 in. (9 cm)

Belted Kingfisher
Megaceryle alcyon
To 14 in. (35 cm)

Rock Pigeon
Columba livia
To 13 in. (33 cm)

Downy Woodpecker
Picoides pubescens
To 6 in. (15 cm)
The similar hairy woodpecker is larger and has a longer bill.

Red-bellied Woodpecker
Melanerpes carolinus
To 11 in. (28 cm)

Northern Flicker
Colaptes auratus
To 13 in. (33 cm)
Wing and tail linings are yellow.

Wild Turkey
Meleagris gallopavo
To 4 ft. (1.2 m)

Sharp-tailed Grouse
Tympanuchus phasianellus
To 20 in. (50 cm)

Greater Prairie-Chicken
Tympanuchus cupido
To 18 in. (45 cm)

Red-tailed Hawk
Buteo jamaicensis
To 25 in. (63 cm)

Turkey Vulture
Cathartes aura
To 32 in. (80 cm)
Note red head and two-toned underwings.

Bald Eagle
Haliaeetus leucocephalus
To 40 in. (1 m)

Barred Owl
Strix varia
To 2 ft. (60 cm)
Call is a loud –
who-cooks-for-you?
who-cooks-for-you-all?

Great Horned Owl
Bubo virginianus
To 25 in. (63 cm)
Call is a resonant –
hoo-oo-oo, hoo-oo.

Horned Lark
Eremophila alpestris
To 8 in. (20 cm)

Purple Martin
Progne subis
To 8 in. (20 cm)

Barn Swallow
Hirundo rustica
To 8 in. (20 cm)
Note deeply forked tail.

Black-capped Chickadee
Poecile atricapilla
To 6 in. (15 cm)
Name-saying call is –
chick-a-dee-dee-dee.

House Wren
Troglodytes aedon
To 5 in. (13 cm)

Tufted Titmouse
Baeolophus bicolor
To 6 in. (15 cm)

White-breasted Nuthatch
Sitta carolinensis
To 6 in. (15 cm)

European Starling
Sturnus vulgaris
To 8 in. (20 cm)

Blue Jay
Cyanocitta cristata
To 14 in. (35 cm)

American Crow
Corvus brachyrhynchos
To 22 in. (55 cm)

Cedar Waxwing
Bombycilla cedrorum
To 7 in. (18 cm)
Red wing marks look like waxy droplets.

Common Grackle
Quiscalus quiscula
To 14 in. (35 cm)

Red-winged Blackbird
Agelaius phoeniceus
To 9 in. (23 cm)

Yellow Warbler
Dendroica petechia
To 5 in. (13 cm)

Baltimore Oriole
Icterus galbula
To 8 in. (20 cm)

Brown-headed Cowbird
Molothrus ater
To 7 in. (18 cm)

American Robin
Turdus migratorius
To 11 in. (28 cm)

Eastern Bluebird
Sialia sialis
To 7 in. (18 cm)

Western Meadowlark
Sturnella neglecta
To 9 in. (23 cm)
Nebraska's state bird.

Lark Bunting
Calamospiza melanocorys
To 7 in. (18 cm)

Bobolink
Dolichonyx oryzivorus
To 8 in. (20 cm)

Dickcissel
Spiza americana
To 7 in. (18 cm)

American Goldfinch
Spinus tristis
To 5 in. (13 cm)

American Tree Sparrow
Spizella arborea
To 7 in. (18 cm)
Note chestnut cap and small breast spot.

House Sparrow
Passer domesticus
To 6 in. (15 cm)

Dark-eyed Junco
Junco hyemalis
To 7 in. (18 cm)

Northern Cardinal
Cardinalis cardinalis
To 9 in. (23 cm)

House Finch
Carpodacus mexicanus
To 6 in. (15 cm)

Virginia Opossum
Didelphis virginiana
To 40 in. (1 m)
Note long fur and naked tail.

Big Brown Bat
Eptesicus fuscus
To 5 in. (13 cm)

Eastern Gray Squirrel
Sciurus carolinensis
To 20 in. (50 cm)

Fox Squirrel
Sciurus niger
To 28 in. (70 cm)
Note large size and bushy tail. Coat may be dark gray, red-brown or black.

Thirteen-lined Ground Squirrel
Spermophilus tridecemlineatus
To 12 in. (30 cm)

Eastern Chipmunk
Tamias striatus
To 12 in. (30 cm)
Note white stripes on side and face.

Norway Rat
Rattus norvegicus
To 18 in. (45 cm)
Brown to gray rodent has a naked tail.

Deer Mouse
Peromyscus maniculatus
To 8 in. (20 cm)
Distinguished by its white undersides and hairy tail.

Black-tailed Prairie Dog
Cynomys ludovicianus
To 16 in. (40 cm)
Tail is black-tipped.

Woodchuck
Marmota monax
To 32 in. (80 cm)

American Beaver
Castor canadensis
To 4 ft. (1.2 m)

Striped Skunk
Mephitis mephitis
To 32 in. (80 cm)

Common Muskrat
Ondatra zibethicus
To 2 ft. (60 cm)
Aquatic rodent has a naked, scaly tail.

Common Raccoon
Procyon lotor
To 40 in. (1 m)

American Badger
Taxidea taxus
To 35 in. (88 cm)

Red Fox
Vulpes vulpes
To 40 in. (1 m)

Coyote
Canis latrans
To 52 in. (1.3 m)

Pronghorn
Antilocapra americana
To 5 ft. (1.5 m)

Bobcat
Lynx rufus
To 4 ft. (1.2 m)

Mule Deer
Odocoileus hemionus
To 7.5 ft. (2.3 m)
Fluffy tail is black-tipped.

White-tailed Deer
Odocoileus virginianus
To 7 ft. (2.1 m)
Fluffy tail is white below and held aloft when running. **Nebraska's state mammal.**